ACKNOWLEDGMENT.

1. Robert DeNiro – His famous outburst on 10th June, 2018 inspired the title of this book.

2. Michael Moore – Movie "Bowling for Columbine". Distributed by:- MGM Distribution Co. Release date - May 16, 2002 (Cannes), October 11, 2002 (United States)

3. Edward Snowden: - Statement on Stuxnet virus that infected Iranian Nuclear centrifuge.

4. *Arabesques$:-* A book written by Ahmed Bansada.

5. Mark Urban – Diplomatic and Defence editor of BBC Newsnight- "Saudi nuclear weapons 'on order' from Pakistan".

6. Micheal Froman - Lead trade negotiator, Obama administration – Trade of Steel with Canada versus China.

7. Metro UK Newspaper – Report on west coast states of USA planning to secede to Canada.

8. Dan Alexander, Forbes magazine – Report on Trump's conflicting interest with a Chinese bank being his most valuable tenant at NY Trump Towers.

9. The Story of My Experiments with Truth - By Mahatma Gandhi.

TABLE OF CONTENTS

Chapter 1

Foreword

When mankind seems to plunge into despair and hopelessness, we often forget lessons from history. The ascent of evil has always been because evil has been conjured and given rise to, for purposes of selfishness and individualistic gains. In darkness and confusion, mankind tends to forget that every tyrant and dictator who ever walked on this earth was loved and adored by his own tribesmen. The primary reason for this attachment for evil is that we are all cavemen by design, thirsting for blood of those who are not like us. In this thirst, we ourselves give rise to blood thirsty warriors of our own clan to decimate and wipe out the ones we don't like. Only when the excesses committed are beyond our comprehension and control, and we observe the world condemning us for the actions of our leaders, do we rise up and attempt to bring them down to avoid any further shame in the eyes of the multitude. But it's far too late, as the battlefield is littered with thousands of innocent corpses slaughtered by our very own desires.

From ancient times to this modern day tyrants have been consistent in their rise to power and their methods of marauding. The main commonality between all of them, right from ancient times, is that they were loved and supported by the masses that kept them safe in power. Be it Nero or Caligula of ancient times to the Hitler and Stalin of modern ages, the only reason they survived their reign is because they were allowed to, by those who revered them. Even medieval conquerors like Genghis Khan are still revered and remembered by their descendants; who take pride in the fact that they created history once upon a time by pillaging and burning down kingdom after kingdom, and mass raping the women folk.

We must all remember though that in when the fires of hell came to earth, there were sparks of light from heaven that gave us hope and belief that the oldest 'War in Heaven' is not yet over and will continue till the end of time. The words of Mahatma Gandhi also hold relevance to the reign of dictators throughout time:

"Remember that all through history, there have been tyrants and murderers, and for a time, they seem invincible. But in the end, they always fall. Remember, Always."

Mahatma Gandhi - The Story of My Experiments with Truth.

Chapter 2

The Obama Era

Before we begin to analyze Trump, we need to step back in time to the start of the Barack Obama era, as that was the primary pre-cursor to the rise of Trump. Many books have been written about him, but the primary points to acknowledge is that Obama stepped up at the time when he inherited the Great Recession of 2008 that hit major countries in the world, with the exception of third world countries like India etc. Many years of war expeditions clubbed with the banking/financial crisis, brought the United States to a grinding halt, where the total national debt rose from 66% GDP in 2008 pre-crisis to over 103% by the end of 2012.

Not only were the Americans angry over such a massive loss to the economy, but also the frequent war expeditions to the Middle East by the previous administrations. American forces deployment to these so called war zones, kept dragging on to a never ending saga draining the US exchequer. Obama's election narratives were well calculated and meaningful in nature, which specifically targeted the real reasons of why US was in that economical crisis. The perfect statesman and a well polished gentleman that he was, he clearly avoided any individualistic attacks on the personal front against anyone, but merely targeted the inefficiencies of the administration into finding a solution to the existing mess.

Obama not only managed to prepare a proper roadmap towards rising from the recessional ashes, but also envisioned and properly prepared the plan for the era post the recession. A large percentage of Americans in 2009 understood the significance of escaping the recession and stood by Barack Obama, as he made sense to them. But the ultra right wing was wary of a black skin person creating history in American Democracy by becoming the first coloured skin president. With nothing to lose they continued their tirade against Obama, as the president continued his efforts in reviving the economy and alleviating the ever mounting debts. Infuriating their fears ever more, was the newly found assertiveness of the African-American community in America, who were now coming out into the open and voicing their opinions. This propelled the fears of the entire white skin race from all sections of society into a corner of paranoia and unwarranted fears of complete obliteration, and who started finding solace in the arms of the 'previously condemned 'ultra right wing factions.

Before the fears of the entire white community are dismissed as unwarranted and baseless, certain facts must be taken into account. From the entire African-American community there is a minority who are the really civilized, welcoming and all embracing types, just like Barack Obama. But, as we start go through video sharing websites on the internet for street violence, the main characters that come into focus are the blacks, who are indeed athletically strong and verbally aggressive. Very rarely would you see a white skin person taking down a black skin person on the streets, in a kerb side encounter. Observing this on ground level on a daily basis can certainly create a fear psychosis in the minds of the passively timid white community. Be it on the streets, in the subway, in public transport, in restaurants and practically everyplace; the more violence one observed from a particular community, the more one is inclined to believe that it's a genetic build-up of that community. These ground level observations also contributed to a growth of insecurity and fear against the Obama administrations, as it was felt that a coloured President only enhanced the aggression on the streets by the blacks.

Obama instantly recognized this fact and realized one crucial element in this fear psychosis. He realized that the more coloured people appeared on television screens, the more it intensified the fears of the white skin races. A black man getting roughly arrested or shot down by the cops did help the white skin man to find relief in those images, but the visuals of black people in the power corridors, only exasperated their fears to a higher proportion. Barack Obama took subliminal prompt action and made sure that majority of his staff and closest advisors were white skin people, responsible for policy decisions and interacting with the masses. This cooled down the fears of the white skin race to a slight margin, but was still wary of a black man at the top of the pyramid in the white house.

Donald Trump the smart businessman was quietly observing this from the sidelines and preparing his red carpet arrival. He did not back then, question Barack Obama's action on foreign and economic policies, as he knew that the American market has to revive with him himself being a victim of the recession; but from time to time attacked Obama on the purity of his birth and the colour of his skin.

Barack Obama has openly claimed that he drew inspiration from Mahatma Gandhi, and the primary philosophy of Gandhi was to get into the mind of the enemy and understand their weaknesses and then act accordingly. Gandhi principle of non-violence has always been misunderstood, even till date. These principles did not state in any way to stand in front of a deranged armed killer and encourage him to pull the trigger. The armed man will do it anyway. The trick was to understand what exactly the person attacking you actually wanted, and either comply with him diplomatically or decline it diplomatically. In both ways, it told the attacker to 'Go to Hell' with a disarming smile, and the attacker looked forward towards the journey.

It seemed that Barack Obama was the only man who really could understand Gandhi's philosophies and at every step of his journey acted accordingly. When Donald Trump attacked him for his origins of birth, he simply responded with the facts and did not indulge in mud-slinging against Trump. Obama knew that direct mud-slinging against Trump back then would only propel Trump as a messiah of the white races, who is at war with Obama's black skin race and bring him instant recognition and fame. This did put Trump into his place who receded into a corner like a reprimanded child; but in a manner where after a few years, during the taking over of the White House it was Donald Trump who felt embarrassed (hidden though) at his past wordplay against Obama, and not the other way around.

But by now, Trump had already become the darling of the right wing factions. White Skin police officers had now gone on a rampage gunning down every suspicious black person, including a 12 year old child Tamir Rice. Obama very carefully did not make any direct statements condemning the police for their actions, as he knew it would have granted the allegations of the right wing group further credibility for supporting the coloured races. While this did hurt the African American community at their president not condemning these incidents, but it did not also gratify the white skin races, who were now craving for more blood on the streets. The People's movement 'Black Lives Matter' did bring this into international focus and the Americans were even happy that it had, as they wanted the world to know that they reject any coloured skin person in the White House.

Obama did carry out his duties passing some landmark bills in the history of America, but Americans were not happy. He was given a second chance at office, although with a lower margin in Congress. Mitt Romney, his runner up to the Presidential race of 2012 was seen to be too weak and liberal towards immigration policies favouring the coloured races and Donald Trump was slowly becoming the favourite of the GOP with his hardened but well calculated racist stance

The ultimate game that Trump played in 2012 was to bow out from the Presidential race. This act of sacrifice was not his typical characteristic, but rather a well played out sympathy strategy. By repeatedly being denounced at by the media for his tirade against Obama's birth origins, it only cornered him into getting further sympathy and moral support from the White Skin races. He did subtly mention that he prefers to go back to his television show, whose popularity was now record high, but also laid the foundations of fear in the minds of White races in America that there is no hope for the country's future and it will always be now ruled by the coloured races. The white races were now even more united in fear and panic at seeing their messiah accept defeat. Little were they to know that this was Trump's strategy to come back with a bang years later.

Politicians around the world have always used the tried and tested method of preying on the fears of the masses. The ones who talk of integrity and brotherhood rarely stand a chance to win, but con the masses into believing that the enemy is at the gates, waiting to invade and they look up to you as their messiah and saviour. In May 2011,

Obama did get carried away and make the mistake of joining the mob in humiliating Donald Trump, when the latter was present at the White House Correspondents' dinner. This was his big mistake and he would pay for it years later.

Barack Obama also from time to time played to the galleries by allying the fears of the Americans, by deriding the Outsourcing industry with the term "No to Bangalore and yes to Buffalo", far back as 2009. While these moves did have a marginal impact, Obama was also sympathetic to the American Industry's needs and did not bring in stringent laws that could have severely impacted American Multinationals giant, who had already suffered due to the 2008 recession. This was also because Obama had still to execute his foreign policies and bring resolution to many outstanding issues, so he perfectly did a balancing act. But Americans were not completely ready to believe him as his skin colour always gave them the benefit of doubt. These actions were constantly lapped up by Donald Trump, who was only using this to prepare his manifesto for the future.

During these years one must carefully analyze that Trump never completely attacked Obama for his policies of bringing back troops from the frontlines and reducing the boots on the ground. Trump being the perfect businessman was well aware that all the years in war had burdened the exchequer and reducing this expenditure would help the economy recover gradually. America's greatest threat Osama Bin Laden was still alive and hiding (or so it was made out to be), and Obama had to still carry out the 'War on Terrorism'. Cost effective drone technology and 'surgical strikes' were the hallmark of the Obama policies that effectively took down Osama Bin Laden in 2011. This definitely helped Obama come back to power in 2012 elections, but it still did not satisfy the masses completely.

Trump being a dedicated Republican always favoured the foreign war expeditions to assert American battle supremacy, but made sure to keep silent about it when it was not needed, acting on popular sentiments. Trump knew how to not criticize against popular measures like Obama bringing down employment rates from 10% to 4.7% in over six years time frame, or passing the $787 billion 'America Recovery and Reinvestment Act' to boost economic growth during the Great Recession or even the landmark normalizing relations with Cuba, while Fidel Castro was still alive. Trump was to learn from all of this and seize his very own 'Cuba Moment' years later.

Trump's attacks on Obama were well calculated and not random or chaotic in nature. He already had the media doing a fabulous job in attacking Obama persistently, despite his performance record. This was again racism in play. The media never liked and will never like a coloured person in the White House. Frankly speaking, the Americans never really preferred a well mannered and civilized president when it came to foreign relations, because Obama was seen as being a very apologetic president during his tenure. Even a simple cultural bow to the Japanese emperor Akihito in 2009 was criticized as being too low and undignified. Americans would rather prefer a President who showed the middle finger to the emperor of a country that it threw the nuclear bomb on, half a century ago. Trump learnt from all of this and made sure to play to the galleries.

Donald Trump effectively used Barack Obama to elevate to power. He did make sure Obama effectively completed his journey and cleared the mess left by his predecessors and prepare for a clean inheritance, but also attacked him using popular fears and sentiments of the White races to project him as the potential adversary of the Black President.

Chapter 3

<u>Trump Rises</u>

In the Hollywood movie 'The Gladiator' starring Russell Crowe, there is a very pivotal scene where Senator Gracchus refers to the Emperor's plan of Coliseum games. He says *"I think he knows what Rome is. Rome is the mob. Conjure magic for them and they'll be distracted. Take away their freedom and still they'll roar. The beating heart of Rome is not the marble of the senate; it's the sand of the coliseum. **He'll bring them death - and they will love him for it**"*.

Consider this in today's global scenario, and it certainly holds ground and is so true to its context. In every society the politician who plays to this theatre of blood is successful and American politicians like Donald Trump, know this very well. Give the Americans prosperity, economic growth, jobs, healthcare and they reject it; but give them blood games and they will love you.

Donald Trump is a perfect businessman celebrity, and knows that the masses need continuous entertainment. Two continuous episodes that do not live up to the expectation of the viewers makes the soap opera lose its sheen and go off air. Who better knows this than Trump, and he knows how to entertain the mob with every episode. Long running television soap operas have unpredictable plots to make the viewer glued to their screens. This is exactly what is going on in America today. The only difference being that this could have long term global ramifications.

Trump's rampage against the Indians, Mexicans, Canadians, Arabs, North Korea, etc may or may not have much substance as compared to the truth, but it does satiate the mobs and reassures them that America is still a global police who has the temerity to rule the world. As I go deeper into why Trump indulged in all this, it will become evidently clear that he is not a racist or some white supremacist, but is merely playing to the gallery to further advance his own needs.

Right from 2008, there were developments working in favour of a man like Trump for 2016. During the 2008 presidential elections, after Obama decimated almost all his worthy opponents, the only one remaining and giving him a worthy fight was Hillary Clinton. The ferociousness and the intellectuality of the debate back then could have easily eaten up a man like Trump, but America was watching this finale very closely. Not only were the Americans wary of a coloured person like Obama becoming the first coloured president in history of America, but also the other contender Hillary Clinton was a woman and the latter would have been even worse than the former in the American patriarchal mindset. The fact that she was from the white race was a little consolation

Obama knew that Hillary Clinton and the Trumps were good friends, and what was going on in the minds of the Americans, so he played a masterstroke and invited Hillary as the first woman 'Secretary of State' in the history of America. This was only to assuage the fears of the masses of a complete coloured invasion of the White House. Now for Trump to be attacking the government on policy issues would have been attacking his close friend Hillary Clinton who was part of the government, so he directed his attacks on Barack Obama's race origins. This was a more convenient and cheaper plot that never fails to entertain the masses.

Trump was picking up key points during the Obama regime, the biggest one being Obama's middle name which was Muslim in nature. During the Obama regime there were shrill voices about Obama being sympathetic to the Muslim Middle east due to his own partial ancestry, and Obama was very careful about portraying this. The fact that it was his government that took down Osama Bin Laden played no consolation to the American public, as Trump later took the opportunity to point fingers at Obama for the creation of the ISIS terrorist organization, which the American gladly lapped up.

Until this time, flirting with Middle East dictators and organizing war theatres in the gulf was mostly seen as protecting American interests and oil investments to secure oil supplies for the future. Although Obama did draw and implement the blueprint for complete energy independence, by encouraging Shale Gas production within America to reduce the dependency on the gulf, his partial Muslim origins were never to be accepted by the white races in America. Obama's Shale Gas program did have a global impact with oil prices crashing to abysmal levels and bringing powerful gulf countries like Saudi Arabia to its knees. However, America was still interested in his skin colour and his Muslim middle name. Trump understood this very well, much better than the others.

During Obama's second term America was prospering, jobs were getting created, Oil prices had crashed, and debts were reducing. But America was not entertained as they found this very boring. The masses needed some excitement and some games, and there was no other person than Trump who was worthy of such deliverance. By now Trump was already a mega celebrity who was making the right political noises from time to time and also propping his image on television. The nation was looking up and was interested.

The time for the 2016 Presidential elections had come, and Obama had no intentions to run for office the third time. He knew the old game of exiting on a high note, and since he had achieved his high note, he thought it prudent of calling it a day. America was now interested to see who could replace the charisma and intellect of Barack Obama. The Republicans fielded 17 candidates (including Donald Trump) and the Democrats 6 (Including Hillary Clinton). Many articles and studies were written on the nominees, and this book does not intend to get into it again. But what was crucial to understand was that America had already decided its finalist; Donald Trump and Hillary Clinton. Every Poll pundit had their bets on Hillary, due to her past experience and her proximities to the White House, and also for her diplomacy and intellect prowess. But, they seemed to have missed out on one primary thing. Donald Trump was already the darling of the masses as he had made the right noises in the last decade, and Hillary was a woman. As in 2008, when America came dangerously close to having the first Woman President of America, the masses would not have it all over again.

The other disadvantage Hillary had was that, she had plenty of international enemies. Her stint as the 'Secretary of State' had already embroiled her in many controversies. Be it handling the Arab Spring Revolution, Benghazi attacks and the taking down of Gaddafi, Syrian Civil war and relations with Bashar Al-Assad, all these were literally put on the platter for Donald Trump who only had to entertain the masses with his inconsequential statements and rhetoric. Condemning and ridiculing him frequently was the biggest mistake of the media and his opponents. According to Gandhian philosophies, *"the final victim in a chain of events gets the maximum sympathy, irrespective of the fact that this final victim may have been the initial perpetrator"*.

America is making the same mistake all over again, by continuously targeting and mocking Trump. It will not be a huge surprise if Donald Trump is re-elected to office again in 2020. This will primarily be the sympathy vote again for a white skin man who tried to portray America as a Superpower in the global arena but was constantly targeted by detractors of American pride and glory.

In 2016, it was quite evident by the way Hillary had lost her debating prowess of 2008, that either she was paving the way for her old friend Donald Trump to get the office by her mild responses to Trump's wild accusations or she indeed had no answers to the tough accusations put forth by the opponents. She did cut a sorry figure and no matter what poll pundits said, Michael Moore's predictions of Donald Trump coming to power was proving to be true.

Leaving aside all the conspiracy theories of Vladimir Putin interference in the 2016 elections, Melania Trump being a Russian Spy, etc., much was already written about Donald Trump's connection to the Russian Mafia and how they repaid him back in 2016. Whether this was true or not may not be consequential in nature without concrete evidence that will never come out, but what was true that many races living in America are from a patriarchal society and would never tolerate a woman in power. Russia is one such place, and Russians in America would never tolerate a woman President dictating terms. Putin being friends with Trump would only advance the Russian side in the Middle East conflict, which was to play out exactly a few months after taking office.

While the media and the other nominees were taking care of Hillary, Trump had to only concentrate on his racial games which he had carefully studied and analysed down the years. There were many factors playing out in the international arena, which had a direct impact on the American Political structure. Donald Trump for some reason was observing all this very closely and acting accordingly. The fool's mask that he puts on from time to time is only to camouflage his real hidden agenda. In politics it is said *"That a joker can make and take the most controversial statement or stance and get away with it conveniently, on account of being accused as a foolish person"*. Donald Trump is one such person, who is very smart and cunning, but who also knows how to camouflage his cunningness and real agenda amidst his madness tour.

The next chapters will get into an in-depth analysis of global international events and the American response to them, paved the way for Trump to construct his manifesto and soothe the hearts and minds of the White Races, thus allowing him to come to power and execute his real agenda. We must remember that Donald Trump has investments around the globe, including countries that he condemns in a well calculated manner. So he does a perfect juggling act of protecting his investments, while at the same time advancing America's racial interests.

Every racial remark that is made is well planned and calculated, and is not some random act of buffoonery. It stems from a well desired need of a certain section of society against another section of society, to protect the former's interests. Trump is only a channel used to voice those opinions and heartfelt issues. Remember the golden lines *"Give the mob blood games and they will love you for it."*

Chapter 4

<u>Indian Americans and Donald Trump</u>

The relation between these two entities is the most complex and intriguing one in existence. The Indian American community are only 1% of the entire US population. According to the '2016 American Community Survey Data', the total population was 3,456,447 (minus all the inter-racial count). While this community might be a miniscule entity who should not possess a major threat to the American fabric; a major psychological threat it did create. Among this entire Indian American population, the Christians are at 1,050,000, but according to Wikipedia's list of notable Indian Americans in US, the Christians total to less than 10. This population was not as significant to upset the political apple cart in America, but their mere presence in the right places was beginning to send shrills of insecurity in the hearts and minds of the European American populace.

The most influential and powerful religious group from this population is the Hindu community. While many of these people may be liberal and secular in nature, the ones that are more concerning are the ultra right wing ideological groups. The group that was accused of having a hand in the assassination of Mahatma Gandhi not only is very much active in USA, but also has an extensive member list operating directly under the aegis of the US Government. Intelligence agencies from time to time have highlighted these groups actively funding their counterparts in India for religious activities. How these funding is used is a mystery, but what is an undeniable truth is that these groups in India have indulged in anti-Christian and anti-Muslim narratives and actions in India.

One would naturally assume that the 'brown-skinned stereotyped' Indian Americans would be aligned to Barack Obama on account of his half-white origins, but the shocking fact is that this community was against Obama. To understand this alignment is extremely complex, simply because India as a society is a deeply divided society on lines of race. The predominant race in India is the light skin ancient Aryans, who had a deep psychological connection to the Nazis of Germany with undisputable evidences of individuals working alongside Adolf Hitler in the 2nd world war. Among the Indian Americans, the Aryans are the ones who are extremely powerful and influential, and consider themselves closer to the white races on account of their own genealogy being light skinned.

The other main adversaries of the Indian American Hindus are the Muslims, due to a 300 year rule   and religious brutalities by Muslim rulers like the Mughal Empire in India. So naturally any white skin politician in America taking a stance against the Muslims becomes a natural ally of this community. Barack Obama did not have this advantage, as his middle name was a suspicious Muslim one and he was not a full blooded white skin politician. This despite the fact that it was during Obama's regime that the Indian American community started getting noticed and entering the corridors of power. Leave alone the federal appointments like US Attorney Preet Bharara who made a lot of noise in persecuting many (non-Aryan) Wall Street suspects; even the world of American business was now noticing the rise of this community. From Satya Nadella taking over the reins from Microsoft's Bill Gates; to Sundar Pichai taking over the reins of search giant Google. There were many other noticeable personalities in the top boards of power, but the reason these appointments mattered is because they happened during the regime of a coloured President. These development naturally gave rise to fears of a foreign invasion and the need for a pure blood white President to stem this rise. Donald Trump was to understand of all these fears, and seized his moment when Barack Obama committed the cardinal mistake in Jan 2015.

In May 2014, India got a new Prime Minister who openly declared brazenly that he is a Hindu Nationalist. Nothing wrong with that at all; except this man was accused of genocide and resentment against the Muslims and Christians in India, which he publicly denied. As a natural course of events, Christian churches became target of vandals and hooligans, who were galvanized by the belief that the top corridors of power will condone their actions and grant them complete immunity.

Fear crept in the hearts of the minority Christians in India as a sign of the time to come.

January 2015, Barack Obama finally broke his silence and voiced his displeasure at the Indian government not taking proactive measures to reassure the Christian community. As was expected, the American Indians Hindus were displeased about Obama projecting their Indian Prime Minister in bad light and vowed revenge. Remember, this was the community that rejoiced in victory on Times Square, when this Indian Prime Minister came to power in May 2014. This was all that a person like Donald Trump needed, who got the opportunity fallen right into his lap.

During the 2016 Presidential elections, few particular groups of Indian American Hindus openly pledged their support for Donald Trump, and he gladly accepted it. Barack Obama had now lost his complete vote bank of the powerful influential Indian American Hindus, some of who saw the power corridors during his regime. In other words, the so called white supremacist Christian Donald Trump had accepted election support from groups who condoned attacks on Christian religious places of worship in India. This went largely unnoticed in America, as the media was mostly focused on bringing down Hillary Clinton that Donald Trump's escapades went off the radar.

Even in India, ultra right wing Hindus venerated and offered special prayers for Donald Trump's victory and celebrated with fervour, went he finally got elected. This only went to prove that Donald Trump is not exactly an inherent racist but a shrewd businessman obsessed with delusions of grandiose and power, and will even strike a deal with the devil to obtain this.

His later actions of coming down heavily on H-1B visas (specifically targeting the Asian Indian software giant's, who were the biggest beneficiaries of this work authorization), were just plain hypocritical white noise. In my previous book 'The H-1B Conundrum', I had exposed how the inefficiencies of USCIS will not result in any practical clamp down of the H-1B visa; but the grey market will only get better at misusing the complex employment grid in USA to maintain the corruption behind this visa structure.

According to CNN report on November 2016, Donald Trump has nearly 16 mega investments in India itself, from his 144 companies spanning the globe. Now surely he is not craving to play Russian roulette with India, all his ultra right wing Hindu supporters, and the wealthy powerful Indian American groups in USA who will just shift their alliances to a Democrat politician at the drop of the hat. Trump's knows very well that the average American is not very intelligent to understand the complexities of politics and only comprehends Hollywood style headlines. Trump is a master of entertainment and creating headlines, and the war against H-1B's is only one such Hollywood blockbuster drama, which entertains the average American.

That this drama did have its effect on ground, when on February 2017 at Kansas, Adam Purinton gunned down two genuinely skilled and talented Asian Indians, mistaking them for Middle Easterners. This was evidence enough that what Trump was doing, was stirring up racial apprehensions simply because the mob craved for it and will love him for doing so.

Chapter 5

The Mexican Standoff

"Refugees are not born, but are created when the marauding horde ravages the land for their own greed and lust for power, and as thus displaces the inhabitants".

Americans should introspect on its own involvement in South American countries to realize the disastrous outcome that has landed on its doorstep. Refugee children being separated from their mothers at the US-Mexican border in 2018 had become an international talking point, and many human rights establishments were already talking about it while voicing their concerns openly. At the heart of it all is US Attorney General Jeff Sessions, who declared that anyone trying to enter the United States illegally will be immediately prosecuted. I only have one simple question to the US Attorney General; what about a person who entered the USA on a tourist visa on fraudulent documents, obtains a legal work permit and now lives a happy life (forever probably)? Important point to be noted here is that the incompetent USCIS and Homeland were informed months in advance, but did nothing about it.

Conjuring high drama at the borders, with weeping children being separated from their mothers is only a psychological game played by the US Government to deter refugees from troubled South American countries. The initial real target of this executive decision by the Trump administration was the Middle East refugees fleeing war torn areas like Libya, Syria, etc. There were reports of these refugees illegally trying to enter USA via the Mexican borders, with help from organized crime syndicates in Mexico.

At this time were also intelligence reports of the now neutralized terrorist organization ISIS, trying to use this route to enter USA and ferment trouble. How this escalated into a South American crisis is for international bodies (if any) to analyze and intervene on time. Donald Trump just like any other opportunistic politician did try to score during the Presidential Elections by tapping into popular anti-Hispanic sentiments. If the world believes that the current US-Mexican border crisis is being condoned by every American with a little conscience, then they are in for a big surprise.

White Conservatives groups look at brown skin children being separated from their mothers as a feast for their eyes, as this satiates their appetite to see brown skin Hispanics being persecuted under the rule of law. Yes, Trump does stand guilty of making profits from these blood thirsty sentiments, and is now in a dilemma to either continue the drama at the border and keep these supremacist groups happy or display his humane side and intervene. The world does not expect Donald Trump to display his intellect strategically like Barack Obama and resolve this crisis, but it sure does need to know that Trump is no ignoramus either and knows how to manipulate his game at attending to policies while keeping the blood thirsty mob happy.

The war between Americans and Mexicans is really as old as the American-Mexican war of 1846, following the 1836 Texas Revolution. Current generation of racist Americans should enlighten themselves with a little history knowledge, easily available on Google. While this animosity has been almost a century old, a new war broke out as late as the 1980's with the Mexican drug cartel.

Mexico may be a producer of narcotics, but it is a major logistics hub for drugs produced in countries like Columbia, Peru, Bolivia, etc. The cartel is so sophisticated and flush with funds that the highly lucrative human trafficking network has also come into their operations. Their major drug clientele is the United States of America, and in return the American Gun Manufacturers supply their best to these cartels. So while there is healthy trade transactions between the two countries, all the election fire drums inciting the mobs seem to be rather hollow, filled with lies.

Various administrations in the past recognized this plague, caused by the Americans itself who fuelled this demand from down south, and trying to educate the Americans is like convincing the devil to accept God as his master. When in 2006, the Mexican government declared an all out war against the drug cartel; the US Administration recognized that it needed to get indirectly involved to assist the Mexican government. Right from the Bush administration to Obama's administration, funds were granted to the Mexican Government, including Military assistance to curb the cartels. The wars were extremely bloody in nature and many deaths (including innocents) occurred all these years, with horrific tales of torture. Obama knew that this had the potential of becoming another Middle East war, as any country who goes to war with USA automatically becomes an ally of almost all terrorist groups fighting America. Leave alone the ideological war, the international drug network is so huge and complex that major governments are involved in it and a plain simple military action will not eradicate it. Mexico has been trying to fight these cartels from 2006 unsuccessfully, despite Financial & Military aid from USA.

Barack Obama recognized one key element here, of the ever growing demand for narcotics in America and finally in 2012 decided to legalize recreational Marijuana. Typical to Obama's style of confronting the issue instead of the person, he did recognize that conceding to the demand for legalizing marijuana in the United States will have an impact on the Mexican Drug Cartel, and statistically it did to a larger extent. Border Patrol did notice a sharp reduction in the Marijuana quantities being smuggled into USA post the legalization.

The war against Illegal immigration and drugs cannot be continued unless Mexico's government is on board, and Trump knows this very well. Sounding hollow drums during elections may be good to win elections, but will it translate into productive outcomes in the longer run? Trump's demand to build a wall on the US-Mexican border and making Mexico pay for it, has already strained relations to a point where Mexico is no longer interested to assist the US Government in tackling the refugee crisis at the borders. Technically, Mexico acts as a buffer for all refugees fleeing politically instable countries in Latin America, and if the US Government is very careful with its relations with Mexico the tide can be stemmed much before the border itself, thus eradicating all the unwanted Human Rights issues currently under the scanner.

But unfortunately Trump with his trumpet had ensured that boat has sailed away long ago, and Mexico is now only happy to let the US authorities deal with this crisis at its borders. Making enemies is extremely easy, but making friends out of potential enemies is an art which Barack Obama excelled at. What went largely unnoticed is that Donald Trump did actually extend help to the Mexican government to smoke out the drug cartels (as if he has the magic formula for that), and according to the Mérida Initiative in 2017 provided the Mexican government $130 million to combat this menace. On April 7th, 2018 Edward Hunt on 'The Progressive web portal' exposing how Donald Trump was secretly funding the Mexican government, and then continuing with his racist chants to please the white supremacist in America.

A silly border wall might or might not curb this crisis, as the drug cartel is not so naive to drive across open plains to America to deliver its goods and has an extensive network of tunnels and underwater transportation system to ensure meet their goal. What needs to be done on an immediate basis is that the International body's attention should be brought to the political instability in Latin American countries and timely intervention needs to happen to resolve this refugee crisis.

Will Donald Trump with his 'Bull in the China Shop' be able to summon the finesse and statesmanship to resolve this crisis? I strongly doubt so, because he knows very well that the Americans would never tolerate a diplomat president; but rather would want someone who is prepared to push the nuclear trigger or indulge in aerial bombings to wipe out all the refugees at the holding camps. The fault here is not of Donald Trump but of the American people who want him to do exactly that.

To exacerbate the problem even further Donald Trump has the 'Elephant in the China Shop'; Jeff Sessions to execute exactly what the blood thirsty mob desires. How does all this affect the global community? There will be a chain effect of those intending to cause trouble to USA, and with Trump on the rampage; the list is now longer than ever. Apart from still active Islamic Terrorist groups and powerful drug cartels around the world, the crisis would be the perfect opportunity to stir a hornet's nest by Latin American insurgent organizations.

America's internal immigration mess itself is so very deep and complex that, that USCIS and Homeland will be so completely stretched out in tackling the border crisis; they will leave the internal grid completely exposed to the sharks within, to manipulate and misuse. What America needs is to strengthen the internal fabric to tackle all kinds of illegal workers and unauthorized stay, and only after that is taken care of the border issue can be easily resolved.

But I seriously doubt the US Administration has the reckoning to weave this torn fabric together and make it tougher without holes. Donald Trump may or may not try to comprehend this situation and how concerning it is, with him being busy in his Hollywood style line deliveries to please the auditorium. The Mexican Standoff is not about the century old war of whites versus Hispanics, but rather a very complex war with many clandestine players involved in it, which are heavily financed and well networked across the globe.

Besides, If Donald Trump's 'Trump Ocean Resort Baja' had worked out successfully; we would be hearing psalms and praises of Mexico from Trump's mouth instead of resentment. It should be clear by now that Donald Trump will never attack any country directly where he has investments. He is a perfect businessman and further chapters in this book delving into the Middle East will only expose how the worst of the lot is actually the most tolerated and pampered child of the west.

The real tipping point for the Americans was to see Mexican filmmakers winning Oscars for blockbuster Hollywood movies. All of a sudden when the African Americans seemed to disappear from the stages of the Academy Awards, the brown skin Mexicans started dominating it. And as old theory goes; when the white man sees too much of coloured men on television, he fears an oncoming invasion of the other races and reacts appropriately. The reaction in America was to vote for Donald Trump to halt this brown skin invasion.

Chapter 6

<u>Outsourced to Mexico</u>

Come elections and every right leaning American politician's favourite punching bag is NAFTA. Implemented in 1989, it commenced bilateral trade with Canada, resulting in the US-Canada free trade agreement. The year 1991, saw the start of bilateral talks with Mexico in the trade agreement. While there have been many opponents of NAFTA, who from time to time presented detailed reports of the exact outcome of this agreement; there was also a major benefit for giant American corporations heavily dependent on manufacturing.

As compared to outsourcing manufacturing jobs to China, Mexico was a better and cost effective option for American companies. Transfer of finished goods was easily done via roadways, instead of the long and expensive seaways, when transacting with other outsourcing destinations. The Mexican government also encouraged the direct entry of American Manufacturers on its soil, through the free trade zones. While all this resulted in greater GDP's and overall economic growth for Mexico, it did result in blue collar job losses in America.

This also reduced (not eliminated) the number of Mexican immigrants trying to enter the United States, as local jobs were now available. The reason it did not eliminate illegal immigrants completely from Mexico, is because of the same old BPO catch; that you ended up earning 1/10th of the wages you would earn in the United States. Earning US Standard wages in USA, resulted in higher remittances back home to Mexico, which many Mexicans did prefer. The Mexican government did vastly encourage the IT/ITES sector outsourcing by developing and incentivising software development industries and projecting Mexico as a complete outsourcing hub in competition with India or China.

But something was looming in the horizon of this economic growth. The war on the drug cartels was taking its toll drastically. The number of violent murders and death of innocents, related to drug wars was impacting the image that the government was trying to create. While the murder rates were not exactly the highest in Latin America, but even a significant number did create a fear psychosis in the minds of potential investors. Mexico had to handle all this whirlpool of drug wars, protecting the near-sourcing industry only to encourage Mexicans to stay back home, and its territories becoming a transit hub for Illegal refugees and Immigrants from Central South America.

Then came along Donald Trump in 2016, who started blaming Mexico for all the evils in America, and the right wing white supremacist took that as music to their ears. Maybe, Trump had his facts corrects, but to him projection is all that matter. Many were ready to support him, as a significant amount of Americans were impacted by Mexico in some way or another. Be it, being a victim of the drug cartel crimes, or losing jobs to Mexico, or simply a fact that the inferior Hispanic race down south of the border were seeing more economic progress than the superpower America; a good lot of Americans were behind Trump to ferment trouble down south only for their pleasure. No one really expected these games to escalate to a level, where the world would now get up and start comparing the camps at the US-Mexico border to the Nazi Concentration camps where children were segregated from their parents.

Donald Trump knows very well that the US-Mexican border wall will serve nothing at all, as the powerful drug cartel has only welcomed the construction of the wall. Is Trump really behind constructing the wall, because he himself is in the construction industry, and via a Front Corporation he could grab the contract for himself once Congress approves of it? Being a shrewd businessman, this is quite likely a possibility. The other reason of reassuring the white supremacist with visuals of a wall keeping the Hispanic races out, may not bring in much financial dividends to USA, but only increase the debt burden. But it would bring him poll dividends by again winning the 2020 elections.

 Politicians around the world are well known for promising the blood of those who are hated the most, but once they come to power, all those promises are never implemented. Voters around the world are not known for their intelligence come election time, because who really comes to power is decided by the Media completely. When the media keeps projecting an issue bearing grave consequence to the security of a nation, it's only natural then that politicians jump up at the possibility of seducing the masses based on that media outflow. No one explained this better than Michael Moore in his movie 'Bowling for Columbine'. Did America listen and learn back then? No, they did not and it's quite likely they will not again this time.

 So visuals of families fleeing atrocities back home, landing up at US Border and facing state sponsored atrocities, may shame the average American as the world now looks at it as a failed banana republic who voted a dictator to power. But in the end, there is a huge covert population that supports what is going on at the US Borders and will reward Trump for this. Mexico on the other hand is having a field day, watching Trump face all the brickbats on the forefront, but if this White House onslaught continues, the world should not be surprised to see the Mexican government enter into an unholy alliance with the cartels and anti-US groups to wreak economical havoc on America.

At the very heart of this immigrant crisis is the drug trade, fuelled by the voracious appetite of the American market itself. After Marijuana was legalized, the cross border trade did have a marginal impact. So now drug cartels have started concentrating on the more potent cocaine and meth. One would be tempted to ask, if sponsoring research in the USA for a substitute of cocaine and meth to meet the local demand would result in a positive outcome? The answers would be quite varied. From rights activists to law enforcement, there would be complete opposition to such an idea. But take into consideration what exactly cocaine and meth does to the body, and how a safer substitute controlled drug at 1/10th the price can produce the same results, without the negative long term side effects and it seems like a long lasting solution to control this unholy human rights mess brewing down in South Central America. The US Government should find a home grown solution to a home grown problem, which has only triggered a complete breakdown of law in developing nations.

In the Hollywood movie 'Inception', there is a scene in Mombasa where a shabby hospital like underground parlour offers people a chance to dream under the influence of a controlled substance. A very profound scene enacted by veteran British actor Earl Cameron, exemplifies why people go under the influence of drugs. When asked *"They come here to every day to sleep?"* Earl replies *"They come here to be woken up"*; *"The dream has become their reality"*.

Maybe it's time that the American government wakes up and realizes that the reason Americans are going under the influence of drugs is because their drugged state has become their reality. If the government really *'wakes up'* it would realize that fulfilling this demand with a synthetic version is the only way to stop international cartels and terrorist organizations attempting to convert global reality.

Chapter 7

<u>The Middle East Belly Dance</u>

The primary and most important information here is that Donald Trump has 8 direct investments in Saudi Arabia; The same country that he blamed for the 9/11 terrorist attack during election campaign. With such a vital interest can his words against the war on terror be ever believed? The answer lies in the simplest of explanation. The Middle East is not a clear cut field with a broad division line. It is the playground of the superpowers, which have thrived on their coliseum games played there. It is of paramount importance to take a brief walk into history to understand how the medieval war of religious beliefs has shaped today's world in the Middle East territory.

The Muslim world is sharply divided into two major denominations of religious ideologies; namely the Sunni and the Shias. Right after the death of Prophet Mohammed his followers descended into a war of who will succeed the legacy of the prophet. Without getting into the details of which is already available almost everywhere, it is most important to note that the same war has carved out the Arab world today, almost to a point where they happily let themselves get played by the superpowers who wish to indulge and carry on with the cold war. Iran today is the de facto ruler of the Shias and Saudi Arabia with the Muslim Holy land under its purview is the leader of the Sunni faction.

America's interests in the Arab world was initially about securing oil reserves and protecting its investors and their investments. Taking into considerations the oldest religious animosities already in place, installing dictators and providing military assistance came as an expected move from time to time. Americans must remember that every Arab villain was once an ally of western powers. America's greatest enemy today is Iran, and everyone conveniently forgets that it was the closest ally of America, during the reign of the Shahs. How relations deteriorated to what they are today is a story widely available everywhere.

The primary reason for conflicts in the Middle-East is because of energy reserves and protecting American Interests and installations in the region. To protect these interests successive US Governments were prepared to take sides and either directly or indirectly indulge in the conflict. Saddam Hussein was an ally of American when he was needed in the war with Iran, but the very second he noticed American Oil companies in Kuwait stealing oil from Iraq's reserves through horizontal drilling, he waged an invasion of Kuwait; thus leading to the Gulf war. Overnight he became a villain of the west who was responsible for every act of Islamic terrorism. Osama Bin Laden was a CIA trained fighter, recruited to fight the invasion of Afghanistan by the Russians. The very second he was abandoned by his political masters he became America's number one enemy.

This entire 'theatre of the absurd's' in the Arab region was always controlled by Saudi Arabia, who with their petro-dollars could drag America to the negotiation table anytime and control the outcome of the discussions. There was another important player in all of this; Israel, who were well connected in the White House and who had to be also dealt with carefully. This entire complex legacy finally fell into the hands of Barack Obama when he took office. Carefully not wanting to take sides, Obama understood the dynamic of the Middle-East and decided to wage an all out diplomatic war on all involved. Some of the decisions taken by the Obama administration were so ground breaking that the Arab world is reeling from its shock

Obama knew that unless America reduced its dependency on Arab oil reserves, the White House would always be dancing to the tunes of the Saudi Royal Family; while completely disregarding the fact that from the 19 hijackers of 9/11 terrorist attacks, 15 were from Saudi Arabia. How did all this take place under the watchful eye of the Saudi Royals? America had to call this bluff soon, else would continue to be the butt of all jokes. Obama with this distinguished political sharpness understood that to launch the political strike on Saudi, he would need to bring down its most powerful opponent, Iran.

Till these times Saudis used to control global oil prices, which the CIA many times in the past had termed as the 'Valve Concept'. When the Saudis wanted oil prices to rise they would bully OPEC to close down the valves and reduce oil supply. Iran had plenty of Natural Gas reserves, but due to the trade embargo imposed on it for pursuing nuclear technology, could not sell it globally. Obama recognized this handicap and tried various methods to bring Iran to the table for talks, much to the delight and amusement of the Saudis, who were not aware of Obama's real intention.

In 2010, a virus called Stuxnet infected the Iranian Nuclear Centrifuge, which was intended to attack Iranian's nuclear enrichment capabilities. As per Edward Snowden, it was the CIA and Israel who had planned this move to bring Iran to its knees, however there will never be any concrete evidence that will come out in the public domain. Was Obama in the know, of this move is unclear; but it did have its intended impact and to what Obama wanted in the first place. In 2015, Iran signed an understanding with the superpowers to limit its sensitive nuclear activities and pursue only clean nuclear energy.

Obama now played the next crucial move with the Iran Deal, where Obama sought to give Iran access to the U.S Financial system. This move while widely condemned was camouflaged so cleverly that very few realized the real intentions of this deal. Although the deal never went through and Obama himself withdrew from the same, its actual intent was met. Iran managed to get access to nearly $100 billion of its assets frozen in the international financial system since the 1979 Iranian Revolution, and that paved the way for it to commence trade with it primary allies. India was one such ally who repeatedly thwarted Obama's move to impose complete blanket sanctions on Iran, as that was the way to keep OPEC and the Saudis under check.

Once Iran was able to flush its natural gas reserves to its primary partners it became a major competitor to the Sunni faction led OPEC community. Obama in the meanwhile had already opened the floodgates of Shale Gas exploration in the American Continent and gas prices in America were not only dropping, but America's dependency on the gulf region were also coming down. All of a sudden with the sudden downpour of fossil fuel easily available globally, the Saudis were no longer in control of its flow and found themselves at the receiving end. Russia too joined in and opened the valves to let their oil reserves be available, and did not concede to the OPEC's demand to keep oil prices at a certain level.

Towards 2014, finally oil prices crashed to an abysmal low, much to the delight of all involved. Obama had finally succeeded in achieving his goal of bring both the warring faction of the Middle East to their knees. Saudi now became an enemy of Obama, and even Iran was not in good books with the Obama Administration due to the Syrian conflict.

During the height of the embargo wars with Iran, Obama knew of Iran's involvement in Syria and Yemen, and although being warned about arming rebel groups in these countries, the administration carried out its agenda. What was born out of this involvement was the ISIS terrorist organization, which initially not only had the support of the Sunni faction countries, but covertly the US administration. Donald Trump got it all right when he accused the Obama government of creating the ISIS group. Only when the world saw what had been unleashed, did they unite and start to bring down this group. Small groups still exist in Europe and will strike from time to time. If the world believes that Saudi is not involved in this, they are in for a big surprise.

Yemen was well under control in the early 2000's; with American ally President Ali Abdullah Saleh controlling the Iranian backed Houthi rebels in the north border with Saudi. A typical US backed dictator flush with US funding, he was despised by his own people. Post the Tunisian revolution; the Obama administration seized the opportunity to covertly fund the Arab Spring. Arabesques$ a book written by Ahmed Bansada, exposes how the western media completely hid the fact from the American public, about the CIA being indirectly involved in the revolution. How that played out ineffectively is for the world to see today. America's ally President Ali Abdullah Saleh was killed by the Houthis when he went to Yemen for a peace deal, Iran backed Houthis control almost the northern half of

Yemen, and American ally Saudi Arabia continuously pound missiles on innocents in Houthi controlled territory in Yemen. Egypt too fell into a failed state, now indirectly controlled by the military, thus crashing their very hopes of pure democracy after dethroning Hosni Mubarak. The Muslim Brotherhood government that took over after the revolution was Qatar backed, and since Qatar (a Sunni nation) was not toeing the line with Saudi Arabia, due to its fossil-fuel based relations with Iran, the Qatar backed Egypt government was instantly overthrown by a Saudi-American backed military controlled government. Qatar did face a backlash by the Sunni nations led by Saudi, by having to face a trade embargo by all Gulf countries.

So while Obama's experiments in the Middle East did have its desired results in terms of Oil reserve dependency, his involvement in the war of terror did have a long term negative impact, which was passed on to Donald Trump. Now the Middle East is such a fractured region that no amount of table diplomacy can reverse the damage already done. Donald Trump had been investing in these countries long before all these events unfolded, and may have hypocritically attacked countries with whom he has good relations with, but it was eventually the American people who decided to bring him in to office, considering all that he promised in his anti-Muslim agenda.

But were this all Trump's anti-Muslim agenda and does he really have an anti-Muslim prejudice? As stated earlier, he is a pure businessman, U.S President or not. The countries that were put on the travel ban list (upheld by the US Supreme Court) were countries that were completely ruined by civil wars, uprisings, or Human Rights violation and had turned into a refugee crisis. Without this ban US would have become an International refugee centre. Not that this ban would do any good, as getting an illegal passport of another country not on the Travel Ban list was very much plausible. But, the already ineffectively worked up and stretched out USCIS and Homeland would not have been able to look into all illegal entries.

Donald Trump knew very well during the election campaign that the Middle East condition was not just bad, but much worse and any amount of meddling any further would only put the US exchequer into further crisis. Considering his actions on Jerusalem supporting Israel demand of making it their capital city, many would have thought its political suicide and would send the region into an uncontrolled conflict. But, Trump had it all cleverly planned out. The one country who could galvanize the entire Sunni fraction to support Palestine was Saudi Arabia, and since Saudi and Trump have excellent commercial relations, Palestine is left all alone seething in anger at the Jerusalem episode. So Trump has in one move pleased both the US ally's, Saudi and Israel.

Now let's look at the biggest threat to global security and the role USA plays in it. This is the Nuclear weapons technology which was used on innocent civilians in Hiroshima and Nagasaki in 1945. Ironically, The United States of America that used it still has the powers to lecture to the world about the manufacture and stocking of this technology. While statistics are openly available about the global stockpile and signatories to various treaties, there are some dark underlying secrets that are completely hidden from the world. Not surprisingly all these secrets are in the within the knowledge of America, and has its consent or approvals.

Two of the world's largest nuclear weapon countries are United States and Russia. The amount of nuclear warheads both these countries have can obliterate the entire world if used In one go. America has 2 major allies in the Middle East; Israel and Saudi Arabia. It's a known fact the Israel has considerable influence on the White House and as such possessing nuclear weapons, after perceiving a threat from the Arab nations should be completely unquestionable. However, the question that never got answered is how all the Arab nations remained silent against this and demand their own right to possess nuclear warheads?

One may be easily convinced that it was influence and constant negotiations by the United States that convinced the Arab Nations to not possess their own nuclear warheads; and that the US would be the primary protector and guardian of the Arab nations in the face of any nuclear threat. This was a complete lie that was thrust on the world. If one were to carefully study the nuclear weapons 'Comprehensive Test Ban Treaty', adopted by the United Nation General Assembly in 1996, which has still not come into force, one would easily deduce the fact that there are 13 countries who are complete non signatories to the treaty.

While Russia has signed and completely ratified the treaty (after successfully testing the 50 megaton Tsar Bomb in 1961), the United States has signed but not yet ratified the treaty. Israel too has signed but not ratified the treaty just like USA, which leaves some rather mysterious questions to be answered. From the 13 non-signatory countries, Saudi Arabia is one of them. Now why would a US ally like Saudi not even sign the treaty and yet not have any nuclear enrichment reactors or have any plans to possess nuclear warheads?

Saudi does treat Iran and Israel as its main adversary, and while Israel already possesses nuclear warheads, Iran was always pursuing this technology (much to the condemnation of the super powers). How it is that not a single Sunni Muslim Arab country, raise their voices against this discrimination? Despite the fact that most of them are flush with petro-dollars in their kitty, they could have easily bullied the superpowers into conceding their demands. *The shocking truth is that Saudi Arabia does possess Nuclear weapons technology*. But, the same is not in their territories or official records. To understand this we need to look at another shocking involvement of the United States in the Middle East; Pakistan.

Pakistan is a natural ally of the United States and its military is funded by the US government from time to time. The pertinent question that Americans should be asking is why does a country that as per common understanding, harboured America's number 1 enemy Osama Bin Laden, continue to be funded by USA? The answer is that Osama Bin Laden was in a US approved house detention, closely guarded by the Pakistani Military and its intelligence agencies ISI. When Osama Bin Laden died of natural causes, the Obama administration staged a very shoddy stage-play to show that a surgical strike killed Bin Laden. The entire drama was so amateurish in nature, that anyone with a little common sense could have understood the truth.

2 Stealth helicopters enter Pakistani airspace without triggering any sort of detection? Were the helicopter operating on electricity that they made no noise? These helicopters hover above Bin Laden home close to a Pakistani Military base, and no one suspects the noise and gunfire and report to the police (close to a military base). The highly advanced and sophisticated seal team have wearable cameras to record this gunfight but this recording was never made public, but years ago the capture Saddam Hussein being arrested in his bunker was well documented and released to the public. One Helicopter crashes, but still everyone in the neighbourhood is asleep and no one calls the police (close to a military base). After the killing of Bin Laden, the next morning the Pakistani government just releases a very tepid response, only to please the Pakistanis. In the end, the world never got to see Bin Laden's body, but years ago did get to see Saddam Hussein being hanged live (as that was not ghastly). Former navy seal Robert O'Neill, who claimed to have delivered the fatal shot at Bin Laden, faced backlash by his former comrades who were part of the operations that night. The fact that although he claimed to have delivered two shots to Bin Laden's head and splitting Osama's head into two, but never knew if the person he shot was Bin Laden or not adds more intrigue to this drama if it was Osama Bin Laden who was killed that night. Again the world never saw the body of the slain terrorist to really get convinced of the authenticity of the operations that night.

The fast is that Pakistan is a front for all the anti-Muslim adventures of the United States. The reason its military is constantly funded by the US government is because it provides highly trained elite killers for operations around hostile territories. Pakistani army is always the shadow behind US ground forces in extreme hostile territories and protecting the rangers and the deltas from direct danger, and the biggest secret of them all; *Pakistan is a repository of nuclear warhead for major Sunni dominated Arab countries*. It is in Pakistan that Saudi Arabia stores its nuclear warhead and in the event of any strikes from Iran or Israel, these warheads will be launched from Pakistan against its enemies. This is the dirtiest secret that will never be revealed to the world.

As per common information, Pakistan will have material for nearly 200 warheads and its common excuse is the threat from India. But how does a country that does not even manufacture its own car or struggle with its economy and social developments, have enough resources to enrich and multiply its warheads to 200 or even more if secret sources are to be believed. The fact is that most of the funding comes from the petro-dollars Arab nations, with the complete consent of United States. On November, 2013 Mark Urban – Diplomatic and Defence editor of BBC Newsnight had written an article "Saudi nuclear weapons 'on order' from Pakistan". This article clearly insinuated that reliable sources had confirmed that the Saudis from time to time had been investing in Pakistan's nuclear program.

It is a shocking fact that the Saudis are dependent on Pakistani Air force pilots to fly their own fighter jets and train their fighter pilots, as their own Saudi citizens are too lazy couch potatoes or flush with petro income to pursue such a boring job of flying fighter jets. The dynamics in the Middle East are far too complex to be divided with a straight line, and all this has been going on far before Donald Trump became President of USA. Yes he was conducting business with all these crafty Middle East players during these times, but which businessman would not in the greed of wealth and fame.

Trump is of course carefully doing his balancing act of playing with the Saudis and Israelis, and will somehow alter the landscape to bring the Saudis to the pulpit, from where they can dictate terms like before, and Obama has warned Trump against doing it. But if this scenario plays out, the only person benefiting financially will be Donald Trump and his family. So he is well in command of the situation and not a raging bull on the rampage.

Chapter 7

<u>The Chinese Dragon</u>

Almost all modern day U.S. Presidents find it attractive to indulge in some China Town bashing during elections, but post elections when reality comes to the table, it becomes very evident that China is a powerful adversary, almost to a point of being referred to by conspiracy theorists as the Biblical Red Dragon from 'The Book of Revelations'. Religion aside, China being the opposite is a very powerful kingdom of this world, and its powers both economic and military have risen to a point where only a powerful group of nations in consensus can dream of challenging it head on.

Almost every strategic and economic expert in America have written detailed essays about the Chinese rise and domination, but the same has failed to reach the average American due to their minute to minute obsession with celebrity lives. This is a weakness that American politicians siege every election and play their manifesto on the uninformed mob.

China as a Kingdom and then as a nation has had its own shares of struggles and challenges, and technically has every right to draft policies for the betterment of their state. Sometimes when greed for power exceeds the need for self sufficiency, countries have gone overboard while dealing with other states in this world. China today as the world's largest economy, is not longer at the negotiation table, but rather controls the negotiation tables around the world.

Donald Trump as a businessman knows every flow of international trade and for obvious reasons will utilize the most provocative information to incite the American public and gain access to the higher office in the US. Apple Computers manufacturing iPhones in China is one such hot topic that is enough to incite the Americans, who ironically rush to Apple stores and wait overnight in long queues to lay their hands on the latest model (manufactured in China). So Americans will vote for a President bashing

China but will happily patronize American brand products manufactured in China. Then how exactly is it the fault of the President of USA?

Ancient China knew International trade better than Kung-Fu, and was a land that gave the world some of the best inventions like Paper, Printing and Gunpowder. The Silk Route also somehow pioneered the term globalization. So it's no surprise that all this ancient knowledge should not flow down to modern day China. This came in the form of manufacturing outsourcing, which the communist government recognized as powerful tools to employ the population, which was the world's largest. The language disability may have taken away its advantage of being a soft skill outsourcing destination, but the Chinese made sure to overcome this disability, by state owned companies directly entering the outsourcing game.

For the while, the west was caught sleeping until the 2008 recession crashed the US markets completely. Only when the world realized that China and India escaped the effects of the recession, did everyone's eyes open to analyze the details. This was the time when America was also making history by appointing an intelligent and smart coloured skin President, who until taking office knew little about the Chinese connection. His erudite background made sure he grasped the entire game quite quickly and acted accordingly without wasting any time, but was it enough?

Establishing itself as an export oriented international manufacturing hub, China had risen to such a position that in 2010 it held approximately $847 billion dollars in U.S Government debt. This in itself gave it considerable powers to negotiate within the US territories itself. As China was America's largest banker, Barack Obama knew he had limited options to take on the dragon, despite making regular election promises to bring the cage the dragon. China literally had the U.S economy in its grip.

One of the main strategies that China adopted was to devalue its currency against the dollar to boost its exports. By giving someone more money for every dollar they bring in to the country encourages the masses to rush to the doors of America and bring back more dollars. This is also a root cause of Immigrants landing up on US Shores. By this time, China's dollar reserves were enough to buy 3-4 African nations if they desired so. Obama wanted to act and put pressure on China to increase the value of its currency against the dollar, but in mid 2010 had to back off from the showdown, when he realized that China's threat of selling off a major chunk of US treasury bonds, could effectively crash the value of the bonds, bringing in another economic collapse in USA.

Eager to recover from the 2008 economic crash, Obama did not take any drastic actions back then. Imposing trade tariffs is a luxury that Donald Trump has now, because the economy has recovered in the two terms of Obama's reign. If Obama had imposed the trade tariffs back then, China could have retaliated sharply causing untold economic misery. The U.S. debt to China was lower than the record-high of $1.3 trillion as of November 2013. This effectively means that USA has to pay up this amount to China, and from where is Donald Trump going to arrange this sum to be able to call the shots with China? In 2017, China's economy produced $23.12 trillion, while the USA produced $19.3 trillion. Until the average American realizes this, no U.S. President in a long time to come could alter this landscape. Donald Trump's so called madness is only to please the mob as he very well knows that the economic trade reality will never dawn on the American public.

Leaving alone economic trade wars, China is very powerful and influential in military and strategic affairs of the world. China's grouse with any country patronizing the Tibetan Dalai Lama is only the precursor for its other relationship parameters with the particular country. USA has openly acknowledged it's friendship with the Dalai Lama and in return can never expect any forgiveness from China for doing so, and the US can easily expect China to be in the Anti-US congregation when it comes to military and strategic affairs.

The North Korea tension is one such covert involvement. Donald Trump wanted his historic moment just like Obama had his while breaking the ice cold relations with Cuba. The only difference was that this time in reality

North Korea was calling the shots and the while the media projected USA as being in complete command of the situation; it was the other way round. North Korea had already tested all the nuclear weapons technology it had to and could now negotiate for a test ban. The world knows it by now, that only after a country has tested its strength in manufacturing and detonating a nuclear bomb, it comes to the table and agrees not to test anymore. The reason is that the respective country now has the tried and tested blueprint to quickly manufacture the bomb, in the face of imminent danger. If the world believes that the North Korean leader will now disarm all nuclear warheads and decommission all enrichment plants, then it's heading for a major surprise. There are many countries that have nuclear warhead banks, and assist countries like North Korea to store them for future use, without the knowledge of the world and completely off the record.

Just as Pakistan is a covert repository for Saudi's nuclear warheads, China or Russia could easily be a safe major repository for North Korean nuclear warheads. The suspicions that North Korean Businessmen conduct legal front operations from Chinese territories, masking the Korean connection, only validates the fact that North Korea has a well established global setup to generate income to fund the Nuclear Program. All this is in complete knowledge of Chinese authorities, but the only reason they allow it is because North Korea is the loose cannon that they need to bully the other south Asian nations into submission. Chairman Mao back in the days may have openly denied assistance to North Korea for a nuclear weapons program, but the two major Communist powers of China and USSR of the days could not really refuse help to a country sharing the same ideology. North Korea did later manage to get help from International bodies to acquire nuclear weapons technology, and China and Pakistan (a US ally) did contribute to this development gradually for something in return. So to completely exclude China from the US-Korea tensions would be foolhardy.

China is a bully of the territory, and that is an undeniable fact. But the main reason why they would indulge in this behaviour is to protect their own commercial and economical interests around the world. Being the world's biggest economical powerhouse it needs to secure every avenue of potential growth; securing their energy reserves or clear access to fossil fuel exporters around the world, China needs to ensure that their transport lines that deliver these needs to satiate their voracious energy appetite is always kept secured and guarded without any obstacles.

Getting a direct access through the territory of Pakistan to gain access to the Persian Gulf or deploying their military might to guard their shipping lines across the Indian Ocean, and even claiming ownership to disputed islands in the South Asian territories is all part of this strategy to gain access to energy and transport lines, only to ensure that their manufacturing and export oriented economy is not stymied in any way. China being a communist country has no religious ideology to spread around the world like the armed Islamists and is least interested in the topics of religion. However, any country patronizing the Tibetan Dalai Lama becomes its natural enemy and would have to face its wrath. Because China cannot directly indulge in an armed intimidation every time it perceives a threat, being an ally with loose cannons like North Korea helps a lot.

Donald Trump in a dramatized show of strength did openly challenge the North Korean regime and threatened war by deploying the USS Carl Vinson aircraft carrier and three other ships in its fleet, to take part in a joint military exercise with allies like Japan and South Korea. It was quite evident that if a war actually broke out, this would have resulted in a global catastrophic chain reaction leading to third world war, but Trump had to do this only to pander to the "2nd Amendment obsessed" American mob who wanted a change from the previous diplomatic statesman like Obama regime, which believed in talks and negotiations. Somehow the Republicans know how to keep the American masses happy at all times with timely theatrics.

While North Korea ran amuck with its tantrums and vitriolic threats directed at USA, it was infact China and Russia (till the Obama regime) that actually backed this behaviour. The US-Russia cold war never ended and is in full swing even today. It may be subdued due to Putin's friendship with Trump's family, but that does not change the China-North Korea equation.

 In reality, even before the Trump administration came to power there were ice breaking strategies adopted by the Obama regime. North Korea was not exactly an iron curtain country under the western educated Kim Jong-un. It allowed visitors from United States to visit its countries, although in a strictly guided tour. US Basketball celebrity Dennis Rodman's trips to North Korea was not exactly to promote or train the country in basketball, but rather as a well conceived plan by the White House to engage with the North Korean leader and break the ice. China of course was very wary of this development as it would have negated its role and authority over the Korean leader, and Donald Trump actually came as a blessing for none other than China.

Trump did have the option to continue with the soft path of diplomacy and resolve the growing tensions, but that is not exactly his image that the Americans voted him for. Having to live up to his image, he took the tried and tested method of hardliner politics that depended on vulgar display of power, wordplay and that he did with great élan to please the coliseum. He calculated his moves very well in this pacific theatre and would not have allowed the tension to escalate to war; as being a businessman himself, he knew of the economic retaliatory strikes that China could launch on the United States financial and banking system. The Singapore diplomatic summit was carefully drafted out in secrecy while preserving his alpha image to the public. So in reality it was the average Americans who wanted this vulgar theatrics of madness, knowing very well that it would result in no major benefits to the American way of life or economy, but merely teaching a motor mouth nutcase like Kim Jong-un a lesson for loose talks.

An elephant ignoring barking canines does not display itself as weak, but as something that understands its own power and might, and what it could really do to the intimidators. A superpower like American (with more than 6000 nuclear warheads) responding to a tiny impoverished country like North Korea, only displays itself as weak and cowardly who can be easily intimidated by practically anyone on this planet. Maybe Americans should really watch repeats of Michael Moore's 'Bowling for Columbine', which so explicitly talks of this inherent fears.

The end result of all this drama ended up in nothing as was expected from many quarters, as North Korea will continue to pursue its nuclear agenda for as long as it sees a threat from the US and its allies. China will continue to protect and guard this nation as it offers something in return by keeping China's adversaries in the South Asian region intimidated. Russia will play a dual standard game, being neutral during the Trump administration and getting back to its aggressive stance if this regime changes in 2020.

Chapter 8

The Canadian Saga

Donald Trump launched a diplomatic war on Canada, because of NAFTA and the American dairy farmers being affected due to Canada's restrictive trade practises. Does America really think that Trump gives a Rat's bottom to American Dairy Farmers? He is least interested in how American Dairy products get treated around the world, as he is a construction businessman and not a farmer.

The world began to think that Donald Trump lost it all, when he declared war on America's closest neighbour Canada, regarding Trade deficits. In simple language this is the difference in billions, when the US Imports more than it exports to Canada. But, remember this is in billions of dollars, not mere thousands of dollars. So has Trump really lost his marbles in talking rough with a country that is its third largest trade partner, from the list of countries that America deals with?

The devil lies in the details, which the average American always seems to miss. America's biggest trade partner is the European Union, China and Canada. In terms of so called trade differences Canada is the least and China has the biggest trade deficit with USA. This means that America imports much more from China than it exports to China. So why the concentration on Canada, when it the least among the biggest partners?

Micheal Froman, a lead trade negotiator from the Obama administration commented to Vox's Emily Stewart on May 31t 2018 that *"Most of the unfair trading that's going on in steel and aluminium is emanating from China, and this action does very little, if anything, to affect China,"* This statement from Michael Froman actually reveals the real story if one were to carefully analyze the hidden ciphers. Europe, Canada and Mexico are not the real culprits behind overproduction of Steel and Aluminium; China is. So why not target China instead?

If readers were to revisit my previous chapter on 'The Chinese Dragon', it would become evidently clear that Trump is actually acting on behalf of the powerful Chinese to curb imports from other countries and facilitate a smooth movement of cheap Chinese steel and aluminium. I have already dedicated an entire chapter on how China is really very powerful and influential in the US financial sector and also in bullying the western powers and allies in South East Asia.

During Trumps visit to China he heaped praises on the country and its people for the 'noble traditions of its people' and the Chinese respectively loved it. But what was going on in reality is a covert understanding of deepening trade relations with benefits for Trump itself. He clearly condoned China for its trade practices and gave the country credit for taking advantage of the U.S on trade. The $250 billion trade agreement signed during this time may have been already negotiated in the past and some of them were non-binding MOU's, but the limelight fell on Trump for this massive trade agreement, and how it would bring jobs to America. Every economist and strategic expert knew that it was all baloney, but Americans loved it because it sounded good on the surface.

China historically is also known to be a big bully, and one wonders if the tensions in the North Korean territory were connected to this trade war drama that Trump staged with America's non-Chinese partners? Whatever 'well calculated' reckless moves Trump did, only benefitted the Chinese in the end, and was this all well planned in advance? If this is so then the great American Lie of being anti-communist got completely exposed.

American has always portrayed itself as a pro-democratic, anti-communist country and went to several cold-war conflicts around the world including Vietnam and Russian ruled Afghanistan. But today when its greatest political partners are Communists and America's real enemies are Democratic countries, one wonders if America is heading towards socialism with Trump wanting to be ruler for life, just like his counterparts Vladimir Putin and Xi Jinping.

The real deal was that US has impressed China to act tough on North Korea and in return US will go soft on proposed trade tariffs and sanctions. China agreed and started to tighten the screws on North Korea, but had completely forgotten history. Just as Chairman Mao had refused to help the current North Korean leader's grandfather with nuclear weapons technology, the latter obtained it from Russia and other western countries. Kim Jong-un was of the same bloodline and did the unimagined, by conducting peace talks with South Korea, which was historic in nature and became global news. Kim Jong-un also signalled that he would be ready for talks with USA, again something that was never imagined in anyone's wildest imaginations. China suddenly felt left out in the cold, with Kim Jong-un's moves and jumped in the picture immediately to assure that they were still in command. But Kim belonged to a particular bloodline that will find new friends upon being threatened by the current ones, and did so exactly. The world saw a powerful Trump finally subduing North Korea, but did not really see that it was the tiny North Korean David that subdued The United States of Goliath.

This was a well calculated move for PR purposes. If a US President can easily subdue a rogue nuclear state dictator, then dictating terms with peaceful democracies would come easy. Canada was one such target in this entire game, but what the world still did not know is the early shrewd moves that Canada was making when Trump was on his election campaign rampage. Justin Trudeau studied the potential of Trump's assault on the skilled immigrants via the H-1B visa issue, and realized it thoroughly that American I.T industries were highly dependent on this arrangement.

So acting swiftly and stealthily, he declared Canada as the next Silicon Valley and started attracting American I.T companies to migrate to Canada. This bonhomie did pay off very well, with Google, Facebook, IBM, Amazon, etc setting up shop in Canada. Also a group called True North offers packages for U.S. companies interested in opening a Canadian branch, with Canada experimenting with looser regulations, tax breaks and rebranding. Ontario's Minister of Economic Development and Growth, Brad Duguid said, "It is not for us to criticize the administration; It us for us to recognize an opportunity when we see it. The current direction of the administration, which appears to look more inward than outward, is in stark contrast to what we believe is the direction we want to go in."

In addition, the Justin Trudeau administration also launched skilled visa programs to attract the current skilled talent from USA to move to Canada. While this could definitely upset the Canadian right-wing factions, who just like any other right-wing factions around the world are xenophobic, The Canadian government will find a solution to ease tensions; as it does not really have a "second amendment" gun crazy culture to deal with. Deranged lunatics running around with automatic weapons are barely heard of in Canada as compared to USA on a weekly basis.

Yes, Canada is very keen on taking advantage of the US conservative rampage against foreigners, and any country in the world would do exactly the same, if given the opportunity. The Tech industry is hurting the most with this rampage and every other major client in USA too. Large corporations in USA have shelved many projects, due to the looming policy uncertainties triggered by the White House. But, is this uncertainty really triggered off by the White House, without the approval of the American masses?

Let's look at another Canadian threat that the Americans perceive as a biggest attack on the integrity and union of the United States of America, so large is this threat that a similar kind of threat was only seen during the American civil-wars. If this threat really exists or is completely manmade is only for analyst to find out, but everything in America runs on fear and sentiments alone. A veteran white man gunning down a coloured skin man was not based on facts but suspicions rooted in fear, and this fear was implanted in his heart by the political establishment and the media.

Post Trump winning the White House seat, many states like California, Washington & Oregon contemplated seceding from the United States of America and becoming a part of Canada. Terms like Calexit and the Oregon Secession Act came into news, because a large number of

Americans not only spoke about leaving America, but taking along their favourite states along with them. While this entire movement may not have been backed or Initiated by the State Governments, but by random groups who feared the outcome of an ultra right wing president taking oath. The very fact that a large number of Americans even considered this move, at the time the 'Anti Trump Movement' was gaining traction, was enough for the entire country to believe that these west coast states were indeed in the process of becoming a part of Canada.

If the anti-trump movement actually failed or not cannot be ascertained, but the very fact that such a group or movement still does exists, makes the supporters of Trump believe that the possibilities of many US states seceding out of USA into Canada, still does exist. In response, Canada is all too amused and happy with such developments, and actually went ahead and welcomed the move if it really gained traction. United Kingdom's highest circulation newspaper 'Metro UK' actually joked about this and called it a perfect solution with Hawaii, Nevada and Alaska also joining ranks and breaking away from USA and becoming a part of Canada. The possibilities of getting Hollywood, Las Vegas as part of Canada would only put Canada on the global map, which USA enjoyed all these years.

Canada may or may not be just a false alarm, but the very fact that Americans have insisted on Trump going on rampage makes Canada look only much better and civilized. The Canadian government must however be on guard to protect its own interests by ensuring that more jobs are created before a mass exodus of skilled immigrants arrives on their shores, or Canada will witness something that it has never in its history; the rise of the right wing insisting on Canada being only for Canadians and an anti-immigrant wave, which will then make America look good in the eyes of the world.

Justin Trudeau seems to be a smart young Prime Minister and could look into the possibilities of soft outsourcing industry that does not come under the trade tariff games, but how will Canada react to this American downhill spiral while still keeping the emotions of its citizens intact, only time will reveal.

Chapter 9

<u>Trump's Trade Tariff Wars</u>

Globally almost every second country practices the concept of Trade Tariffs, to ensure that the goods do not over flood the markets and crash the price barriers. Every manufacturer reserves the right to make a profit from what they make and sell, and if a country has a particular trade or goods to sell to the world, they would want to ensure that their own manufacturers have an advantage over any foreign companies. This is called mild protectionism.

There are beliefs that protectionism has its roots from socialism or otherwise popularly condemned as communism. Most communist countries have state sponsored industries that manufacture all the nation's requirements, and insist on its people only buying these goods. This ideology stems from the policy to ensure job creation for the locals, by the state involving itself in everything. How this has resulted in the end is there for the world to see with the biggest example of ex-soviet bloc countries.

The other side of protectionism is the harsher method, where countries impose a prohibitive trade tariff on goods or services from another country, simply because they do not share good political relations. So if Cuba were to impose a prohibitive trade tariff on American goods, it's simple because of its clashing ideologies which almost resulted in both countries coming on the brink of a nuclear war during JKF's regime. If carefully analyzed it would seem that Donald Trump is indulging in a mix of both, and the Americans seem to love him for it, without understanding its long term implications. If Trump has a hidden feelings for socialism is not known openly, but his admiration for communist dictators and their style of functioning is well known.

It is a well known fact that Trump is a perfect businessman and naturally will have investments in the stock market across the industry spectrum. One of Donald Trump's portfolios is Apple Computers and Trump invested in it well at a time when Apple used to outsource its manufacturing to China, so therefore Trump criticising it now is a bit hypocritical. The Outsourcing of iPhone manufacturing to China resulted in better profits for Apple, and respectively its shareholders like Donald Trump. Would getting the manufacturing process back to America ensure the same level of profits for Apple or would the higher cost of production affect its profits, is for time to tell. But, will Trump be willing to continue holding his Apple shares were the profit margins to fall, is an amusing event the world would like to see.

It seems to be clearly evident that Trump again does not give a rat's bottom to Americans getting jobs or anything, but merely to make sure that his own investments remain safe and profitable. During the Presidential campaign, Trump set the bogeyman among the public in the name of NAFTA and Trans-Pacific Partnership. Now the TPP as a trade agreement was only drafted by 12 countries during Obama's reign, but in reality was never ratified or rather came into force. No country was forced to sign the agreement in any way, but the Americans loved to be terrified and Donald Trump was only happy to oblige. He made the NAFTA and TPP look as if it were attacking the very foundations of American Democracy.

The real reason the TPP was conceptualized by Barack Obama was to check the rising dominance and bullying tactics of China in the Pacific region. If one were to carefully check the list of countries in the partnership, it would become evidently clear that they were at some point bullied by China. The very fact that China was never part of this partnership makes it even clear that they were the real intended target of this partnership. One of the covert understandings of this partnership was the easy flow of arms and war technologies, should a war breakout with China. It would become easier for USA to keep a check on China through this method.

This was the thorn in Trump's foot, as he has excellent relations with China. The 'Industrial & Commercial Bank of China' is his most valuable tenant Trump Towers, New York. Dan Alexander of Forbes magazine reported on February 28, 2018 of the conflict of interest hidden in plain sight. It is a common known fact that almost all banks in China are state controlled, which means that the Chinese Government is Trump's tenant, and who would want to lose such an important tenant by signing on an agreement like the TPP that was designed to keep a bully under check. Trump did exit the partnership in 2017, but for some mysterious reason on April 13th, 2018 said the United States may rejoin the Trans-Pacific Partnership. Does rejoining the partnership now not affect American interests?

The countries that Obama sought to keep control of on the international platform are in reality Trump's closest friends, and it should seem obvious now, were the ones who were backing Trump to the White House by ousting Obama from it. When Trump announced that America will go to war with ISIS, the world rejoiced but could not see the fine print. Trump also said that he will then ensure that Exxon Mobil will then ensure control of the oil flow from those regions instead of ISIS. Donald Trump has shares in Exxon Mobil, so if Exxon makes a profit so does Trump.

Donald Trump is not an imbecile bulldozer on a rampage. He is a well calculated and crafty man who knows how to use the American public for his own profits. As a free trade country, when America imports its goods it pays by American dollars. The more countries it pays by dollars the more important the currency becomes in international trade. Countries like India are dependent on its Diaspora (Indians working abroad) to send back foreign remittances to India. These so called remittances are nothing but American dollars which India needs to buy goods and services from other countries. The dollar apart from the British pound and the Euro is a very important currency for international trade. By becoming an export driven country as Trump wants America to be, USA will earn in foreign currencies thus reducing the importance of the dollar.

China is technically the world's largest export driven country, but there is no scramble for the Renminbi, which is China's national currency. China earns in dollars and other currencies and its foreign reserves are very high. Theoretically, America has more control over a nation who has maximum of dollars in its reserves. The currency wars have been known to be more powerful than conventional wars of guns and bombs. An entire nation can collapse on the brink of poverty due to these non-conventional wars. America got a taste of it in 2007-2008 and may get a chance once again if Donald Trump goes ahead with his agenda in totality.

Trump is well aware of these dynamic, or atleast one should hope he is. But he knows it too very well that talking to the American public about this is like preaching the bible to the devil. He is a celebrity showman and knows exactly what to tell the public when they want it. Will Trump take America to the path of so called Socialism only time will tell, but it has been proven without an Iota of doubt that pure Socialism has failed completely. China has realized this long ago.

Chapter 10

The Real Story

America is a sharply divided society today. There are the liberals who are extremely embarrassed at a man like Donald Trump being their president, but there are the conservatives also who always wanted a man like Donald Trump at the helm of affairs. Donald Trump is exactly who he is; a result of his upbringing. He lives his lifestyle unabashedly because he can afford it, is entitled to it and sees no wrong in it. Trump was a natural born businessman who thinks and acts that way, and like every other American aspired to become President of USA, which after several attempts finally achieved his dream.

The world would never have been concerned if Trump had to take office from an outgoing incompetent white skin president, but instead he took control of the White House from a much polished, intelligent and dignified but hated black skin president. The world saw how America reacted when a coloured skin man took over office in 2009. The white skin race came together in fear, foreseeing domination of the coloured races. The law enforcement authorities went on a shooting rampage killing black men under suspicion, there were wide spread hatred for anything coloured and every time a coloured skin person came on TV or in the movies the fear intensified. From African Americans coming in the limelight to Mexican filmmakers winning Oscars, America could not bear it any longer to see the decimation of the white man.

There was a silent retaliation going on, with the Academy Awards not nominating a single African American during those years, foreign students getting gunned down in university campuses by mentally depressed vagabonds with automatic rifles in their kitty, Indian Americans coming under attack for apparently stealing American jobs; the list just continued on showing the world that America as a society still wanted its old racial segregation days.

The whole world is a patriarchal male dominated society where women are treated as the biblical 'Man's Rib' and America is no different from the rest. The only person who could possibly take on Trump was the intellectually gifted Hillary Clinton, but she was a woman trying to enter into an office reserved for men and America would have none of it. Hillary Clinton was the old fashioned conservative housewife who did not divorce her husband Bill, when her husband had transgressed with another woman; but years later when she presented herself as an independent modern thinking strong woman who was capable of taking over the White House, Americans questioned her real intentions of not walking out on her husband when he committed adultery. She was suspected of being ambitious and having greed for power by staying with her then 'President of USA' husband. The patriarchal odds were already against her even before she started campaigning.

Barack Obama on the other hand presented himself as a supporter of woman's right, advocating the need for a modern independent woman, when he offered Hillary Clinton the 'Secretary of State' position. This is something that society could accept, as she was still under the rule of a man, irrespective of the designation. In comparison, the United Kingdom seemed to be much ahead in its way of thinking when it gave a chance to a woman to be its Prime Minister, or even for that matter a third world country like India in the 1960's.

Donald Trump may be accused of several immoral indulgences, but to be honest he is entitled to it. Never has he ever sworn to be a celibate monk, or even renounce his worldly possessions. He was raised to be money and power aspiring individual, who should indulge in everything that it can buy. So if a porn actress like Stormy Daniels came along and accused Trump of indulging in something that she wilfully delivered, Trump supporters were least interested in her story. She offered a service and she was adequately paid for it, and Trump's second wife Melania should have nothing to complain about as having a title like 'FLOTUS', comes with the package. And besides she did ouster Trump's first wife from the frame, and should have known that a man who is capable of treating one woman as a used tissue paper is capable of treating the remaining too.

The fact is that America adores a man like Donald Trump, simply because he is a White alpha male, he is an open misogynist, belongs to the conservative belt society which believes that a woman's place is at home. The heart of America is the so called conservative Bible belt, which believes in every word of the bible. Gays, lesbians, women's right, right to abortion, don't-ask-don't-tell, or anything condemned in the bible is not acceptable to this society. Any politician advocating these causes is likely to be thrown out of politics. However a celebrity rising to the stars and becoming America's national Icon simply by releasing a sex tape is very much accepted by the conservative belt, reason being that the Bible considered Mary Magdalene to be a prostitute, accepted by Jesus. So a woman being a prostitute, offering carnal favours to the President of USA is a well accepted norm of society, which is why all the misconduct allegations against Trump will have no political consequences at all.

Xenophobia or the fear of foreigners resides in every human right from pre-historic times, and even today man is no different from the cave men. We all fear the outsider coming into our clans and disrupting our ways. America is no different in any way, as the west coast hates the east coast and vice versa, Texans hate all non-Texans, etc. So the entire American country hating the coloured skin immigrants should not be any different. American pilgrims actually went to war with the Native Americans after landing in their new home, so this war is as old as pre-historic times. But if this war with outsiders escalates to a point of bloodshed and killing, then we as humans have not evolved from the cavemen.

What really exasperates the fear of the Americans is the Immigrant coming and becoming more successful and powerful than the locals itself. Italian Immigrants evolving into powerful mafia clans makes them despised; Indian Americans arriving in hordes to take over American jobs gets the locals angry and one day all this is all set to burst out in the open. For America the time came in 2016, in the form of Donald Trump who did not really relate to all these fears, being born with a golden spoon in his mouth and having traded with all races and creeds around the world; but knew how to capitalize on the fears of the Americans. He has mastered his art so perfectly that he can convince the Americans that he is concerned about their rights, but craftily takes care of his own commercial rights, and the public either cannot understand it or is willing to look away from it. Just as long as Trump keeps spewing venom on America's most hated, he will be loved ardently by his countrymen.

Let us also not forget the contribution that the media made to the rise of Trump. Today this same establishment is constantly bringing him down, but in 2016 it pampered him and raised him to the pedestal, thus convincing America that the messiah has arrived to deliver salvation. There is an old saying, of course inspired by the bible, that "If you live by the media, you will die by the media". So the same media that brought him up in 2016 is seeking to take him down, because the world looks down at America at the choices it has made in its rampage. But the media might be fighting a losing war, as to bring Trump down it needs a replacement on the pulpit, and right now it has no one who can talk sense into America. The society is seduced to believing that salvation will come when all the foreigners are thrown out of the country and "America only buys American".

Will covert socialism/communism come into play? As words like 'jobs for locals' has been the main agenda of communism right from the heydays of this ideology. Communism was needed to overthrow the oppression that imperialism caused, but ideally after stabilizing the country democracy should have been established. As communist government continued with their inward protectionism policies, it sent their countries into utter poverty and a complete collapse of the social order as communist thugs started calling the shots on the streets. It did create fashionable dictators, who did only replace the emperors and kings of imperialism days sending their countries spiralling back into hell. America needs to be extremely cautious of this path.

Protecting jobs of the average American is fine, but putting a gun to the head of industries has traits of communism. American Industries need to be incentivised for hiring locals, with better and more powerful rights than the employee itself; else the entire game will come back full circle. The US government needs to understand the realities of why American industries prefer cheap immigrant labour, outsourcing and find a middle ground for both employers and employees for better job creation. Donald Trump may be an excellent businessman, but not a clever strategist like Barack Obama to be able to find a middle ground and bring both parties to the table for talks.

Trump will indulge the masses in precisely what they want as he prefers being a celebrity showman and businessman later, but authoritative moves do always have repercussions which will affect the economy badly. Making iPhone in America is an excellent idea, but Apple not making profits due to the high cost of inputs will send the company into ruins and that is not a good idea as competitors will be more than glad to crush American goods with cheaper and much reliable goods. Lessons from Japanese cars entering America should never be forgotten. At first they were laughed and mocked at, but when America finally realized that the smaller imports were much more reliable and efficient, it crashed the local car industry.

America today is on a path where there are no choices available to replace the head of state. The ones who love Trump will vote him back to power until it really begins to feel the after effects of the shocks created, and then in desperation will vote for someone like Obama who will be constantly condemned for not being of a pure European decent with a bible background. The ones who hate Trump will constantly be in search of a worthy opponent to take on the hypocrisies and expose the realities, but will such a worthy contender be found on time is a real challenge.

Until such time, whether you love Trump or Loath him, please do analyze him carefully.